Original title:
Glacial Stars

Copyright © 2024 Swan Charm
All rights reserved.

Author: Kaido Väinamäe
ISBN HARDBACK: 978-9908-1-0499-7
ISBN PAPERBACK: 978-9908-1-0500-0
ISBN EBOOK: 978-9908-1-0501-7

Embracing the Void of Winter's Night

In twilight's glow, we gather near,
Laughter sparkles, hearts sincere.
The world draped in shimmering white,
We dance beneath the frosty light.

The stars above twinkle and gleam,
Warming spirits like a dream.
Hot cocoa swirls in festive cheer,
As we embrace what we hold dear.

Snowflakes whisper, soft as air,
Winter's beauty everywhere.
With every smile, the world ignites,
Filling our souls on this cold night.

Together we weave tales delight,
Under the soft, enchanted night.
In winter's void, we find our grace,
Creating warmth in this sacred space.

Chilled Reflections in the Milky Way

Stars twinkle brightly, in the velvet night,
A cosmos alive, with shimmering light.
Snowflakes dance gently, with joy in the air,
Echoes of laughter, everywhere to share.

Galaxies swirl, in a festive ballet,
Colors collide, in a beautiful display.
Mirrored in ice, the universe glows,
A celebration of wonders, as winter bestows.

Harbingers of the Winter Cosmos

Winter brings magic, with each chilly breeze,
Frosted whispers, rustling through the trees.
Celestial bodies, align with delight,
Gathering warmth, through the cold, moonlit night.

Each star a story, of friendship and cheer,
As the cosmos cheers, drawing loved ones near.
A blanket of stardust, wraps the world tight,
In winter's embrace, all hearts feel the light.

Icy Nebulas Illuminate the Dark

Nebulas glisten, like diamonds in flight,
Sprinkling the darkness, with joy and bright light.
In the depth of winter, their colors ignite,
A tapestry woven, in the deep starry night.

Each comet that passes, brings dreams on its tail,
Carrying wishes, like a shimmering trail.
In cosmic wonder, we find our way home,
Under icy vaults, together we roam.

Crystalline Visions in the Firmament

Visions of crystal, in the night sky unfold,
Stories of warmth, in the freeze of the cold.
Fireworks of starlight, burst with delight,
Painting the heavens, a joyous sight.

The heart of winter, beats with vibrant flair,
As people gather, their voices fill the air.
Celebrate moments, under celestial sway,
As crystalline visions, light up the way.

Starry Spheres Adorned in White

Under blankets of shimmering light,
Gathering joy in the soft moon's bite.
Laughter echoes in crisp, cool air,
As warmth unfolds in the night so rare.

Children dance in a flurry of snow,
Spreading magic in their playful flow.
Stars glisten bright in the velvet sky,
While dreams take flight, and spirits fly high.

The Silence of Frosted Orbs

Frozen whispers in the quiet night,
Frosted orbs gleam with gentle light.
The world stands still, wrapped in a trance,
Nature holds its breath, in a festive dance.

Candles flicker and shadows play,
Inviting warmth on this chilly day.
Hearts grow fuller, and smiles unfold,
In the silence, memories retold.

Celestial Frieze of Frozen Light

Skyward wonders cast a spell so bright,
A celestial frieze of pure delight.
Twinkling stars weave a fabric divine,
Together we share in this festive design.

With cups raised high, we savor the cheer,
Laughter rings through as loved ones draw near.
In this tapestry woven of dreams,
Joy is the thread that endlessly beams.

A Reverie in Ice and Twilight

Twilight dances with a cool embrace,
A reverie in time, a magical space.
Icicles glisten like chandeliers bright,
Catching glimmers of the fading light.

Whispers of laughter and songs in the air,
Celebration blooms beyond compare.
Hold tight to moments, the sweet, the bright,
In this festive wonder, all hearts unite.

Icy Veils Over Celestial Shores

Beneath the stars, the night does gleam,
Icy veils dance like a dream.
Waves of frost caress the shore,
Whispers of joy, forevermore.

Laughter rings in the frosty air,
Hearts ablaze without a care.
Moonlight twinkles on frozen seas,
A festive spirit on the breeze.

Celestial Ice and the Twilight's Glow

Celestial ice, a wondrous sight,
Glowing softly in the night.
Twilight wraps the world in peace,
Festive feelings never cease.

Beneath the stars, the laughter swells,
In icy realms where magic dwells.
Joyful gatherings, spirits ignite,
As hearts mingle in pure delight.

Shattering Silence Under Frozen Skies

A hush falls o'er the snowy land,
Frozen skies, so close at hand.
Laughter breaks the shattering peace,
In moments where worries cease.

Twinkling lights like stars on ground,
In this festivity, love is found.
Every heart a melody sings,
Underneath the joy that winter brings.

Luminous Frost Under Astral Canopies

Luminous frost, a sparkling dance,
Underneath the stars, we prance.
Astral canopies unfurl wide,
Inviting all to join the ride.

With every breath, we radiate cheer,
In this frozen realm, love draws near.
Together we shine, a bright array,
In festive hearts, we find our way.

Luminous Echoes from the North

Stars twinkle bright, in the evening light,
Joy fills the air, as laughter ignites.
Winds dance through pines, a soft serenade,
The night whispers secrets, in a colorful parade.

Footsteps on snow, a rhythm divine,
Hearts beating loud, in sync with the time.
Fires crackle near, casting warm glow,
Festive spirits rise, in the shimmering snow.

Beneath a Veil of Snowlight

Blankets of white, on the ground befall,
Echoes of joy, in the night's soft call.
Candles aglow, illuminate the way,
Bringing together, both night and day.

Children's delight, in the frosty embrace,
Snowmen arise, a whimsical face.
Songs fill the air, harmonies blend,
Beneath starlit skies, we twirl and we mend.

Glimmer in the Arctic Skies

A canvas of night, with colors so bold,
Auroras dance freely, a sight to behold.
The chill kisses cheeks, with a laughter so bright,
As warmth fills the hearts, on this magical night.

Mirthful together, we spin 'round the fire,
Sharing our dreams, and hopes that inspire.
Each flickering flame, tells a tale of delight,
In the glow of the moon, everything feels right.

Frosted Radiance of Distant Worlds

Crispness in air, a sparkling delight,
Gloves on our hands, holding warmth tight.
We gather as one, under twinkling stars,
Lifting our spirits, forgetting our scars.

Frosted branches gleam, in the soft evening glow,
Stories exchanged, as the soft breezes blow.
With every soft laugh, and every warm cheer,
We celebrate peace, as the season draws near.

Celestial Ice and Night's Caress

In the glow of twinkling lights,
Joy dances on the air,
Snowflakes twirl with pure delight,
Each one a whispered prayer.

Under stars that brightly gleam,
Laughter echoes far and wide,
Fires flicker, shadows beam,
As hearts embrace the tide.

Children's giggles fill the night,
Wrapped in warmth, a cozy snug,
Glittering dreams take glorious flight,
With every sparkle, a loving hug.

Beneath the celestial caress,
Winter's magic we embrace,
In this festive wilderness,
Together, our hearts chase.

Cosmic Crystals on a Winter's Breath

Amidst the frosty, sparkling scene,
Cosmic crystals in the air,
Glistening like hopes unseen,
In every breath, we share.

Joyful souls drift and play,
With cheeks aglow and bright,
Every moment, a holiday,
In the heart of winter's night.

Candles flicker, warmth ignites,
Hot cocoa brings sweet cheer,
Laughter lifts the chilly sights,
In melodies we hold dear.

Together, we weave a tale,
Of magic, wonder, and delight,
With every breath, we set sail,
On a cosmic winter's night.

Luminescent Frost and Stellar Serenades

Beneath the canvas of the night,
Frosty hues in every hue,
Starlight twinkles in sheer delight,
As dreams unfold anew.

Luminescent glow surrounds,
Whispers of the festive cheer,
As nature's beauty astounds,
In the crisp atmosphere.

Carols rise, a soft refrain,
Echoes 'neath the moonlit glow,
Joyful hearts, free from pain,
In harmony, they flow.

Underneath the frozen stars,
We gather close, hand in hand,
Celebrating near and far,
In this enchanting land.

Celestial Crystals in the Night Sky

Celestial crystals paint the dark,
With shimmering trails that sing,
A night alive with joyous spark,
   As festive spirits take wing.

Winter's breath, so soft and light,
Carries laughter through the trees,
As we gather 'neath the starlit flight,
   In the cool, inviting breeze.

Fires burn with stories told,
As the night unfolds its grace,
Hearts aglow, both young and old,
   In this magical embrace.

With every twinkle in the sky,
We find hope and love anew,
Together, let our spirits fly,
In a world where dreams come true.

Frozen Constellations

Stars awash in brilliant light,
Twinkle joyfully tonight.
Each a gem in velvet skies,
Whispers dance where magic lies.

Snowflakes drift like feathered dreams,
Laughter echoes, joy redeems.
Children play in frosty air,
Hopes and wishes everywhere.

Glistening paths through forests roam,
Hearts are warmed, we've found a home.
Fires crackle, tales ignite,
Embodied by this starry night.

Bonds of love in chilly gleam,
Wrap us in their festive theme.
Together in this winter's spell,
Frozen constellations tell.

Ethereal Fragments of Night

In the stillness of the night,
Moonbeams cast a silver light.
Twinkling stars like diamonds rare,
Fill the world with whispered air.

Magic swirls in winter's breath,
Echoes of delight, not death.
Each moment glows, a fleeting chime,
Ethereal fragments caught in time.

Joyous rhythms fill the space,
Laughter dances in this place.
Hot cocoa warms our chilly hands,
As we cherish what life stands.

Frosty nights and hearts so free,
Together here, just you and me.
In every fleeting, stolen glance,
Ethereal dreams weave our romance.

Shimmering Icebound Dreams

Glittering snow, a magical sight,
Whispers of dreams take flight.
Sculpted arches, crystal bright,
Shimmer beneath the pale moonlight.

Families gather, spirits soar,
Echoes of laughter we adore.
Frolicking under the silent sky,
Hope and warmth as moments fly.

Candles flicker, hearts ignite,
Binding us to this festive night.
In icy realms of purest grace,
We find a warm embrace in this space.

Wishes float on frosty air,
Radiating joy from everywhere.
Shimmering dreams, forever bright,
In this winter's starry light.

Celestial Fractures in the Frost

Celestial wonders paint the night,
Frosty shards of pure delight.
Every breath a sparkling song,
Together here where we belong.

Glistening trees stretch toward the sky,
Nature's beauty, oh so high.
Each moment filled with warmth and cheer,
As friends gather, drawing near.

Glimmers of hope through darkest cold,
Stories of warmth and joy retold.
Children's laughter, the sweetest sound,
Celestial fractures where love is found.

Beneath the stars, our worries cease,
Wrapped in the night's tender peace.
Frosty tales in a world so vast,
Cheers to the present, forget the past.

Night's Glimmering Crystals

Stars above, like diamonds bright,
Illuminate the frosty night.
Each twinkle sings a joyful song,
Inviting all, where dreams belong.

Laughter dances on the breeze,
Flowing softly through the trees.
Children play in coats of warmth,
Their smiles shining, love's true charm.

Candles flicker, colors blend,
As hearts converge, joy has no end.
In every shadow, sparkles bloom,
Chasing away the winter gloom.

Together, under the lunar glow,
We weave our tales in soft, white snow.
With every heartbeat, echoes cheer,
In night's embrace, we hold dear.

Cosmic Frostbite

In the stillness of the freeze,
Galaxies spin with playful ease.
Twinkling stars with a frosty bite,
Invite us to dance in the night.

Crystals form on windows bright,
Painting patterns, sheer delight.
Under moonglow, our spirits soar,
Each step carries joy to explore.

Echoes of laughter, sweet and clear,
Wrap us warmly, close and near.
Hours drift by, we sway and glide,
In this festive, chill, we abide.

Beneath the cosmos, hand in hand,
We explore this winter land.
With every twirl, the stars unfold,
Magic in the cold we hold.

The Chill of Astral Whispers

Whispers float through the frozen air,
Secrets shared, no burdens bear.
The starry sky is our canvas bright,
Painting dreams in silky night.

Fingers trace paths on icy panes,
Reminding us of joyful gains.
Glistening light on cheeks aglow,
We embrace the frosted flow.

Through foggy breaths, our voices rise,
Carried high to the starlit skies.
Each laugh, a note of festive cheer,
In every heart, love draws near.

Layered coats and bundled bliss,
Every moment, a frosty kiss.
Together, we share this grand delight,
In the chill of the starry night.

A Dance in the Icy Void

In the depths where cold winds play,
We find warmth in a bright ballet.
Steps of joy upon the frost,
Celebrate what cannot be lost.

Twinkling lights from above descend,
Drawing hearts that never bend.
Snowflakes swirl like joyous dreams,
In the air, laughter gleams.

Shivers warm as bodies sway,
In our hearts, the ice gives way.
Every spin a tale untold,
Beneath the sky, our spirits bold.

Round and round, in a merry throng,
We dance together, spirits strong.
A festive rhythm fills the void,
In every beat, love's joy deployed.

Stars Buried Beneath a Frosted Expanse

Twinkling lights in the night sky,
Whispers of joy as they glide by.
Snowflakes dance in playful delight,
Covering all with their purest white.

Laughter echoes through the trees,
Beneath the branches, a gentle breeze.
A world of wonder, bright and bold,
Where stories of winter are lovingly told.

Candles flicker, their warmth aglow,
Gathering friends as the cold winds blow.
Hearts are lifted, spirits arise,
Under the watch of a million skies.

Here we find warmth, here we find cheer,
In the embrace of this festive sphere.
Stars above and joy below,
In a frosted realm, we dance and glow.

Ethereal Glow of a Frozen Canopy

Beneath the trees, a shimmer bright,
Glistening softly in the night.
The world adorned in crystal lace,
Nature's splendor, a warm embrace.

Twilight sings with a soft caress,
As frost ignites the earth's own dress.
Each branch a jewel, each leaf a star,
A fairy tale spun from near and far.

Children giggle in the moonlight's grace,
Making memories in this sacred space.
With snowball fights and sleigh rides near,
Laughter and glee fill the frosty sphere.

In the stillness, our hearts unite,
An ethereal glow, a festive sight.
As we gather close, warmth and delight,
Beneath this frozen canopy, pure and bright.

Dreamlike Ice and Galaxies Unseen

In a world of ice, dreams take flight,
Galaxies dance in the shimmering light.
The night is alive with magical views,
Where time forgets, and hearts renew.

Skating on lakes, under the stars,
The cosmos twinkles, erasing our scars.
With every glide, our spirits soar,
In winter's embrace, we long for more.

Whispers of snowflakes fill the air,
Promises born in the chill we share.
A bond forged in laughter, bright as the moon,
Echoing gently, a festive tune.

Around the fire, we swap our tales,
With warmth in our hearts, as the new snow hails.
Under the blanket of cosmos so vast,
We cherish the moments, forever to last.

Hearth of the Cosmos Under an Icy Blanket

Gathered close by the flickering flame,
The hearth of the cosmos calls our name.
Under an icy blanket, we find our peace,
In this wondrous night, our worries cease.

The stars above seem to wink and play,
As night embraces the end of the day.
Chasing shadows, they dance and swirl,
Filling our hearts with joy, like a pearl.

Snow drifts gently, like whispers in air,
We share our dreams, our hopes laid bare.
With mugs held high, we toast to the night,
In this festive glow, everything feels right.

A tapestry woven with stars and light,
Each moment treasured in this pure delight.
Together we revel, with spirits so bright,
Under the cosmos, our hearts ignite.

Frigid Luminescence and Cosmic Sighs

Beneath the shimmering stars, we cheer,
The winter's chill brings warmth so near.
Dancing shadows in the frosty glow,
Whispers of joy in the crisp winds flow.

Candles flicker in the silver night,
Meaningful laughter, hearts feeling light.
Glistening frost upon every tree,
In this magic, we are wild and free.

Songs of the cosmos, a lovely tune,
Under the watchful eye of the moon.
Sparkling wonders in each breath we take,
With every moment, new memories make.

In this festive dream, let spirits soar,
Together we gather, forevermore.
Frigid luminescence, in hearts we find,
A cosmic sigh, with love intertwined.

Night's Embrace in a Frozen Realm

In night's embrace, the world is still,
Kissed by a frost that gives a thrill.
Twinkling lights like stars descend,
Creating magic that will never end.

Around the fire, stories spun,
Each laughter shared, a cherished one.
Cozy blankets wrapped so tight,
Every heartbeat a festive delight.

Snowflakes dance in the moonlit air,
Painting a canvas with tender care.
With every step, the world aglow,
We celebrate all that we know.

In frozen realms, where dreams unite,
Festive hearts bring the world to light.
A symphony of joy, pure and bright,
In night's embrace, our spirits ignite.

Illuminated Ice in a Darkened Dream

Illuminated ice beneath our feet,
Crystalline wonders, a festive treat.
As shadows whisper tales of delight,
We gather close on this magical night.

Stars above with a twinkling grace,
Reflecting warmth in this frosty space.
Children's laughter fills the chilly air,
Joy and wonder beyond compare.

With every snowflake, a secret told,
In a world where the heart turns to gold.
Together we dance in this dream so bright,
Illuminated ice, a beautiful sight.

In the stillness, our wishes rise,
Painting the canvas of winter skies.
With hearts entwined, a festive blend,
In this darkened dream, may joy transcend.

Whispering Lights Amidst the Frost

Whispering lights twinkle on high,
Gentle flickers like a soft sigh.
Amidst the frost, the world aglow,
Painting our dreams in a radiant show.

Carols echo through the winter air,
Voices rising, a melody rare.
Golden laughter amid silver trees,
In this moment, we're bound to seize.

Each gift shared, a story unfolds,
Ember warmth in the winter's cold.
Beneath the stars, our spirits sing,
In whispering lights, we find our wings.

So let us gather, hand in hand,
Together we stand, a festive band.
In the embrace of this frosty night,
Whispering lights, our hearts take flight.

Chilling Luminescence in the Heavens

Stars twinkle bright in icy air,
A dance of light, a cosmic fair.
Winter's breath, a gentle sigh,
In frosty silence, dreams pass by.

Snowflakes swirl like fairy dust,
Each flake a wish, a whispered trust.
Beneath the moon's soft silver glow,
The world adorned, a sparkling show.

Crisp laughter echoes, joy takes flight,
As hearts unite on this festive night.
Together we gather, warmth we share,
In chilling luminescence, beyond compare.

Ethereal Nightfall in Crystal Form

Evening falls with grace untold,
Wrapped in blankets of shimmering gold.
Frost-kissed branches, bright and fair,
A magical scene beyond compare.

Bubbles of laughter float in the air,
As we celebrate, full of care.
Frozen crystals weave their lace,
In the twilight's warm embrace.

Candles flicker, shadows play,
As vibrant voices soar and sway.
Under starlit skies we roam,
In this ethereal night, we feel at home.

Frozen Celestial Whispers

In the hush of night, whispers glide,
Celestial tales of joy and pride.
Frosty winds carry songs of old,
In a world where warmth can't be controlled.

Moonbeams dance on frozen streams,
Lighting our hearts and filling our dreams.
Echoes of laughter, bright and clear,
In this moment, we hold dear.

Nature's beauty in glistening hues,
A tapestry woven with laughter and views.
Beneath the stars, we find our way,
In frozen whispers, we celebrate today.

Glistening Lights Beneath Ice

Beneath the ice, a world aglow,
Glistening lights in soft undertow.
As the night wraps us in its arms,
We dance beneath its shining charms.

Each sparkle tells a story bright,
Of love and laughter, pure delight.
In the quiet, hearts align,
As joy flows sweet like aged wine.

Through layers of frost, our spirits soar,
Festive vibes we can't ignore.
In glistening lights, we find our cheer,
Under the stars, the night feels clear.

Crystal Glows in the Arctic Night

In the hush of icy whispers,
Stars shimmer in a glowing sea.
Moonlight dances on frost-kissed skies,
A crystal dream, wild and free.

Joyous laughter echoes softly,
While snowflakes twirl in merry flight.
Each breath a cloud of winter's breath,
In the arctic night, pure delight.

Beneath the aurora's vibrant arcs,
Nature's canvas comes alive.
With each flicker, hearts ignite,
In this realm where wonders thrive.

Festive lights on frozen trees,
As the world takes pause to cheer.
In the night, magic enfolds us,
With love and warmth, we draw near.

Shining Through the Icebound Quiet

In the stillness of the evening,
Glows a warmth that fills the air.
Icicles shimmer, bright and vibrant,
Illuminating moments rare.

Joyful spirits wander through,
Making memories by the fire.
Each glowing ember tells a tale,
Of dreams and hopes that never tire.

The stars are diamonds on the ice,
Painting stories with their light.
Families gather, hearts entwined,
In the soft embrace of night.

With laughter ringing clear and true,
We share the magic of the hour.
Together in this frosted space,
We bloom like winter's brightest flower.

Celestial Ice and the Ethereal Night

Beneath a blanket of snowy white,
The universe unfolds its tale.
Celestial wonders overhead,
In the silence, visions sail.

Each flake a whisper from above,
As dreams ignite like fairy fires.
Frosted branches twinkle bright,
In this night where hope inspires.

Festivities whisper through the air,
A dance of joy in silver light.
With every sound, the heart takes flight,
In a realm where spirits unite.

The atmosphere hums with delight,
As we celebrate our shared plight.
In the embrace of the cosmic sea,
We shine together, you and me.

Specters of Light in Frosted Skies

In the distance, shadows glimmer,
Specters of light begin to play.
Frosted winds carry laughter,
As night embraces the day.

With each twirl of the northern breeze,
Stars join in a glowing race.
Magic dances on icy streets,
As joy lights up every face.

Festivals spring from the cold ground,
Hope ignited, hearts ablaze.
In this wonderland of dreams,
We cherish the fleeting craze.

So let us gather, hand in hand,
Underneath the vibrant glow.
In the spectacle of the night,
Together, we shall joyfully flow.

Twilight Aura and the Frigid Firmament

Beneath the stars, the laughter glows,
A canvas bright where joy bestows.
Frost-kissed dreams in twilight's hold,
Warm hearts unite as stories unfold.

Candles flicker with a friendly cheer,
Whispers of love we hold so dear.
The moonlight dances on the snow,
As joy and magic start to grow.

Galaxies twirl in the winter's night,
Gathered souls in a festive light.
Each smile shines with a radiant spark,
As echoes of laughter fill the dark.

Together we stand 'neath the shimmering sky,
With dreams and wishes that float up high.
In this moment, so pure and clear,
The twilight aura draws us near.

Celestial Gleam on a Winter's Breath

In the hush of night, the stars ignite,
A celestial gleam, pure and bright.
Snowflakes twirl like dancers on air,
Underneath the moon's gentle stare.

Fires crackle, warmth from inside,
Laughter spills forth, hearts open wide.
Each moment cherished, time stands still,
Full of joy that the season will fill.

Chimes of joy in the winter breeze,
We gather around like buzzing bees.
With arms interlocked, we face the cold,
Creating memories worth more than gold.

Every glance shared, a story told,
Moments like these are treasures to hold.
In the embrace of the frosty night,
The world feels perfect, cozy and right.

Radiant Threads Against the Frost

Bright colors weave through the snowy white,
Radiant threads against the frost's bite.
Hand in hand, through the glistening dawn,
We dance as if the chilly air spawns.

Vibrant laughter fills the frozen air,
Every voice sings without a care.
Hot cocoa warms our fingertips,
As we indulge in sweetened sips.

Candles in the windows softly glow,
Signaling warmth as the chilly winds blow.
Gifts exchanged with smiles and glee,
Each moment treasured; together we be.

In the tapestry of winter's embrace,
Love wraps us tight, a warm, soft space.
With radiant threads, we light up the night,
Together, shining boldly, all feels right.

Echoes of Light in a Frozen Sea

In the silence of night, echoes play,
Beneath the starlight, dreams drift away.
A frozen sea glimmers, pure delight,
Reflecting laughter, hearts feeling light.

Branches bare twinkle with festive cheer,
As whispers of joy draw loved ones near.
Crisp air sings with an age-old tune,
Inviting us back, a joyous commune.

Skating upon the ice, spirits soar,
With every glide, we wish for more.
Snowflakes fall like confetti from skies,
Each one a blessing, a sweet surprise.

In this dance of light, we find our place,
Sharing warm hugs in the frosty space.
With echoes of love in the vibrant night,
Together we bask in joyous light.

Shards of Light in the Polar Night

In the stillness of the night,
Shards of light begin to dance.
Colors swirl like dreams in flight,
A celestial, twinkling chance.

Joyful laughter fills the air,
As snowflakes twirl and pirouette.
Families gather without care,
Creating memories we won't forget.

Fires crackle, warmth so bright,
Stories shared with hearts aglow.
In this winter's pure delight,
Together, love continues to grow.

Stellar Tapestry of the Frozen Realm

Underneath the starry skies,
A tapestry of dreams unfolds.
Whispers of the night arise,
In this realm, where wonder holds.

Snowflakes drift, a gentle grace,
Wrapping the world in quiet cheer.
Each twinkle, a soft embrace,
A reminder that joy is near.

Neighbors gather, spirits high,
With mugs of cocoa, sweet and hot.
Laughter echoes, hearts will fly,
In this frozen, festive spot.

Ghosts of Frost Kissing the Sky

Hushed streets glimmer, secrets bright,
Ghosts of frost dance on the breeze.
They twirl and sway, a wondrous sight,
Whispers of joy among the trees.

Carols sung with voices clear,
Echo through the chilling night.
Children's laughter brings us near,
In this season's pure delight.

With every heart, the warmth ignites,
Creating bonds that hold us tight.
Underneath the frosty lights,
We celebrate love's shining light.

Whispered Legends of the Cold

In whispers, legends softly sing,
Of frosty nights filled with delight.
The tales of old begin to cling,
To hearts aglow in soft moonlight.

Candles flicker, shadows play,
As stories weave through chilly air.
Families gather, love will stay,
In shared warmth, they find their care.

With every glance, a spark ignites,
Reminders of the love we share.
Together we embrace the nights,
Creating magic everywhere.

Chilling Light Between the Stars

Under the sky's twinkling delight,
Festive dreams take their flight.
Bright lights dance in a cosmic swirl,
As magic unfolds in a joyous whirl.

Night unfolds with a charming glow,
Each star's shimmer starts to flow.
Whispers of joy in the chilly air,
Bringing warmth beyond compare.

The universe sparkles, laughter ignites,
Colors explode in merry sights.
Together we gather, hands held tight,
In the presence of this festive night.

Hearts swell with the wonder we share,
In the chilling light, we dream without care.
A tapestry woven of light and cheer,
Under the stars, we hold each dear.

Ethereal Night and Icicle Dreams

Ethereal night draped in white,
Icicle dreams capture the light.
The world twinkles with frosty cheer,
As laughter rings through the chilly sphere.

Crisp air filled with a vibrant song,
Where joys and spirits truly belong.
Frost-kissed whispers float on air,
Each snowflake dances, a beauty rare.

The moonlight plays, a radiant guide,
Inviting us out with arms open wide.
Together we weave through the snowy lanes,
As joy encapsulates our snowy plains.

A canvas bright, our spirits take flight,
In this ethereal night filled with light.
Icicle dreams melt sorrows away,
Creating a festival in joyful array.

Icy Hues in the Stellar Night

Icy hues paint the vast expanse,
Inviting hearts to join the dance.
Under a blanket of shimmering stars,
We celebrate life, no matter the scars.

The air is crisp, filled with delight,
As shadows play in the pale moonlight.
Colors collide in a frosty embrace,
Uniting us all in this joyous space.

Soft laughter echoes through the trees,
As we share tales carried by the breeze.
Radiant moments, love intertwined,
In icy hues, our hearts aligned.

Together we bask in the night's embrace,
Each gentle smile brightening the place.
Icy hues twirl under the starlit sky,
A festival of warmth that won't be shy.

Aurora Whispers in a Frozen Space

Aurora whispers dance in the dark,
Lighting up dreams with a vibrant spark.
Every twirl adds a festive cheer,
As magic blankets the world we hold dear.

Frozen space covered in glow,
Colors mingle, a stunning show.
The soft embrace of a winter's night,
Wraps our hearts in sheer delight.

Laughter echoes, bright as the dawn,
As shadows retreat, the spirit is drawn.
Together we stand, hand in hand,
In this moment, forever planned.

With every pulse of the cosmic stream,
We join the dance, lost in the dream.
Aurora whispers sing to the skies,
In frozen space, joy never dies.

Frosted Skies and Astral Whispers

Under frosted skies we gleam,
Stars twinkle bright, like a dream.
Laughter dances on the air,
Joy and love are everywhere.

Candles flicker, warm and bright,
Gathered souls in soft moonlight.
Whispers carry on the breeze,
Hope and cheer from trees to leaves.

Snowflakes twirl like confetti,
Each moment feels so ready.
Hearts unite in merry song,
In this magic, we belong.

With every smile, spirits rise,
Frosted beauty fills our eyes.
Together we embrace the thrill,
Of festive nights, our hearts to fill.

Winter's Slumber Under a Celestial Veil

Winter's slumber, soft and clear,
Beneath the moon, we hold dear.
A celestial veil drapes the night,
Embracing us in pure delight.

Crystals glisten on the ground,
In this wonder, peace is found.
Fires crackle, laughter bright,
Echoing into the night.

Hushed whispers in the cold,
Tales of joy and warmth unfold.
Each heartbeat, a festive tune,
In the glow of a silver moon.

Together round the hearth we gather,
In this warmth, our hearts do tatter.
With every story shared, we see,
A winter's night in harmony.

Glimmers of Hope in Frosted Shadows

In frosted shadows, glimmers shine,
Whispers of hope, divine and fine.
Laughter spills like gentle streams,
Filling hearts with vibrant dreams.

Beneath the trees, soft snowflakes twirl,
In this dance, the spirits whirl.
Wrapped in joy, we find our place,
With smiles that time cannot erase.

Cups are raised to friendship true,
In every heart, the joy we strew.
Frosted breath in the chilly air,
A festive spirit truly rare.

As night descends, the stars ignite,
Guiding us through the winter's bite.
We find our warmth, hand in hand,
In this magical, frosted land.

Cosmic Shimmers on a Frozen Canvas

Cosmic shimmers dance above,
In the stillness, we feel love.
Frosted canvas, pure and wide,
Holding dreams we cannot hide.

Under stars, our spirits soar,
Each moment, we seek for more.
With every joke and every song,
This festive night, we all belong.

Snowflakes weave a shimmering thread,
As laughter echoes, joy is spread.
In the chill, hearts grow warm,
Wrapped in light, we face the storm.

Celebrate through every cheer,
In this moment, feel no fear.
With cosmic glows to guide our way,
We revel in this starry play.

Glittering Ice and Forgotten Dreams

Upon the lake, the sun does gleam,
A tapestry of winter's dream.
With laughter high, the children play,
As sparkling frost marks their ballet.

The branches wear their crystal crowns,
While joy in every heart abounds.
In every flake, a wish bestowed,
As sunlight dances, carefree flowed.

The chill embraced by warmth and cheer,
Echoes of joy, the season near.
With every breath, the magic glows,
In dreamy realms where wonder flows.

As twilight falls, the stars ignite,
A symphony of pure delight.
In ice and light, our hopes take flight,
In glittering dreams, the world feels right.

Astral Fragments in a Frozen Sea

Beneath the veil of frosty skies,
The world aglow, a feast for eyes.
With whispers soft, the night unfolds,
A canvas where our dreams are told.

The moonlight dances on icy shores,
As laughter echoes, adventure soars.
Each star a gem, a wish in flight,
In frozen sea, we chase the light.

With every breath, the air is bright,
The warmth of hearts in starry night.
Together we weave stories bold,
In astral dreams, our joys retold.

As dawn awakens, colors bloom,
Dispelling shadows, chasing gloom.
In frozen realms, we find our peace,
In every heart, the joys increase.

Ethereal Glimmers and the Cold Void

In realms where shadows softly sway,
Ethereal glimmers light the way.
With every step, our spirits rise,
As joy unfolds beneath the skies.

The cold void whispers secrets deep,
While dreams like diamonds wake from sleep.
The laughter shared, the night aglow,
In every heart, a spark to grow.

With every flake, a story spun,
In frosted fields, our lives are one.
As evening falls, we twirl and dance,
In dreams of magic, lost in chance.

Together in this wondrous night,
We chase the glimmers, pure delight.
In the cold void, love's warmth we find,
In every heart, our hopes aligned.

Shimmering Frost and the Silent Sky

Beneath the moon, the world aglow,
Shimmering frost in whispers flow.
With every breath, the magic sings,
As winter's charm on soft winds brings.

The silent sky, a canvas wide,
Where dreams take flight, and joy abides.
With every twinkle, spirits soar,
In frosty realms, we seek for more.

The trees adorned in crystal grace,
Reflecting light on every face.
In fragile beauty, hearts unite,
With laughter bright, we greet the night.

With stories shared and wishes bold,
In shimmering frost, new tales unfold.
Together here, our spirits rise,
In festive warmth beneath the skies.

Luminous Frozen Dreams Unfold

In the night where snowflakes dance,
Laughter echoes in a merry trance.
Twinkling lights in the cold air gleam,
As we gather close, sharing a dream.

Joyous hearts illuminated bright,
In a world wrapped in sparkling white.
Together we laugh, together we cheer,
Creating warmth in the winter's sphere.

Each breath creates a frozen mist,
In this festive moment, we persist.
With every hug and every song,
Our spirits unite where we belong.

So let the stars in the frosty skies,
Guide our smiles and joyful sighs.
For in this season, magic unfolds,
In luminous frozen dreams we hold.

Celestial Frost and Cosmic Threads

Beneath the stars, the world ignites,
With silver frost that dances bright.
Each one drapes the earth like lace,
A cosmic tapestry taking place.

Glittering snowflakes swirling high,
In the chilly embrace of the night sky.
Warm hearts gather to share delight,
Underneath the celestial light.

Laughter mingles like shimmering stars,
As we celebrate the warmth from afar.
In winter's breath, our spirits soar,
With love and joy forevermore.

So let us weave these threads of gold,
In the chill of night, together we hold.
With celestial frost sparkling anew,
In this festive joy, we find what's true.

Spangled Ice and Starry Reflections

Reflections glimmer on the icy stream,
Where the night whispers of a dream.
Spangled ice beneath our feet,
With every step, our rhythms meet.

In the stillness, joy takes flight,
As sparklers light the snowy night.
We gather close, hearts entwined,
In this festive warmth, love defined.

Watch as the stars add magic's touch,
To this moment we treasure so much.
With joyous echoes, laughter rings,
As we celebrate what the season brings.

So let the lights begin to twirl,
Through shimmering frosts, our spirits swirl.
In spangled ice, we find our way,
In starry reflections, we choose to stay.

Night's Chill and the Luminous Unknown

As night descends with a frosty sigh,
The world sparkles beneath a velvet sky.
In the chill, there's warmth to be found,
Where laughter of friends paints the ground.

Under stars, we dance with glee,
In a moment that feels so free.
With twinkling lights to guide our hearts,
Creating bonds that never depart.

The luminous unknown ahead does gleam,
Filling our souls with a shared dream.
In the night's embrace, we face delight,
With joy alight in every sight.

So let us cherish this festive cheer,
As the chill warms with those we hold dear.
For in the night, our spirits glow,
In the festive dance of the frozen snow.

Winter's Light Beneath a Starry Veil

Snowflakes dance in merry glee,
Glowing softly, wild and free.
Candles flicker, warmth ignites,
Winter's magic, pure delights.

Laughter echoes through the air,
Friends and family gathered there.
Songs of joy fill every space,
Hearts entwined in this embrace.

Twinkling lights on branches sway,
Colors burst in bright display.
Fires crackle, stories told,
Memories made, treasures bold.

As the night wraps gently round,
Love and laughter can be found.
Underneath this starry sky,
We embrace the night, oh my!

Frozen Echoes of Distant Worlds

In the hush of winter's glow,
Whispers of the past we know.
Stars align, a cosmic dance,
Hopes awakened, dreams enhance.

Ice crystals form on windowpanes,
Nature's beauty, here remains.
Joyful hearts in twinkling lights,
Celebrating festive nights.

Snowmen stand with smiles so wide,
Children laughing, hearts open wide.
Gifts exchanged with love and cheer,
In this season, oh so dear.

Through the chill, our spirits rise,
Magic glimmers in our eyes.
Frozen echoes of delight,
Sparkling stars shine in the night.

Chilling Serenades in the Cosmic Vastness

Winter nights are filled with grace,
Serenades from outer space.
Melodies the stars create,
Echoing through the frozen state.

Wind and snow, a gentle tune,
Harmonies beneath the moon.
Joyful hearts, they spin and sway,
As the night melts fears away.

Each note floats through frosty air,
Carried forth, a treasure rare.
Dreams connect like stars up high,
A celebration as they fly.

From the depths of winter's chill,
Charming whispers, soft and still.
In the vastness, love ignites,
A festive warmth on these nights.

Stars Like Crystals in the Chill

Glistening stars on icy ground,
Nature's jewels, pure and profound.
Each shimmer tells a tale of grace,
Lighting up the cold embrace.

Frosted trees, a sparkling sight,
Dancing softly in the night.
Children's laughter fills the air,
Joy and wonder everywhere.

Sipping cocoa, warm and sweet,
Gathered close, where hearts do meet.
In the glow of twinkling lights,
Celebration shines so bright.

As we share these moments dear,
Filling every heart with cheer.
Winter's magic, pure and still,
Stars like crystals, hearts to fill.

Dreaming in Sleet and Stardust

In the hush of twilight's grace,
Sparkles dance in frosty space,
Laughter mingles with the chill,
Sleet-kissed dreams, they linger still.

Underneath the silver skies,
Wishes float like fireflies,
Hearts aglow with winter's charm,
Wrapped in love, safe and warm.

Whispers of a joyous choir,
Ignite the night with pure desire,
Stardust falls, a gentle gift,
In this time, our spirits lift.

With each step on snowy ground,
Festive echoes all around,
Dreaming deep in night's embrace,
Magic sparkles, we find our place.

Frozen Galaxies in Winter's Embrace

Beneath the stars so crystal clear,
Galaxies of joy draw near,
Frosted paths where children tread,
Echoes of the tales we've read.

Chilly winds with laughter blend,
A warming heart, the chill can mend,
Mirthful moments twirl and sway,
In winter's arms, we dance and play.

Snowflakes whisper secrets old,
Of stars and dreams, a tale retold,
In every flake, a story spins,
Of festive cheer, where joy begins.

Frozen lights like diamonds gleam,
In the night, we dare to dream,
Underneath this cosmic show,
Warming hearts in winter's glow.

Phosphorescent Whirlwinds of Ice

Around us swirls a storm of light,
Phosphorescent dreams take flight,
As ice confetti fills the air,
With every spin, we shed our care.

Lively dances through the snow,
In a world where bright dreams flow,
Each twirl a spark of joy we weave,
In winter's breath, we dare believe.

Glittering skies of frozen beams,
Whirlwinds wrapped in silver dreams,
In laughter's echo, we unite,
Basking in this joyous night.

From icy depths, the colors bloom,
Bringing light to every room,
Together, we'll forever glide,
In phosphorescent waves, we'll ride.

The Arctic Canopy's Velvet Glow

Underneath the velvet sky,
Auroras dance and spirits fly,
With every hue, the night ignites,
A canvas filled with festive sights.

Frosted trees like sentinels stand,
Guiding hearts and joining hands,
In the crisp, cool evening air,
Magic whispers everywhere.

The snowflakes sing, a gentle tune,
As stars align to bless the moon,
Each moment shines, a treasure grand,
In winter's warmth, we take our stand.

With every cheer that warms the night,
In the Arctic's glow, we find our light,
Together as one, let's celebrate,
In this festive realm, we resonate.

Frosted Nebulas and Winter's Breath

Frosted whispers in the night,
Stars twinkle with delight.
Lights dance in the frosty air,
Magic lingers everywhere.

Laughter fills the chilly sky,
Joyful hearts and spirits fly.
Snowflakes swirl like gentle dreams,
In this world, nothing's as it seems.

Voices rise, a festive cheer,
Gathered friends, all dear and near.
Warmth ignites through winter's chill,
In this moment, time stands still.

With each breath, a spark ignites,
Celebrating wondrous nights.
Underneath the frosted glow,
Winter's love begins to flow.

Silent Echoes Beneath the Ice

Silent echoes softly call,
Beneath the ice, where shadows fall.
Frosted trees wear crowns so white,
Echoing joy throughout the night.

Candles glow in the frigid air,
Spreading warmth, a loving care.
Voices hum a melody sweet,
As winter's magic fills the street.

A dance of light, a swirl of grace,
In this hush, we find our place.
Under starry skies, we're free,
Holding onto memories like a dream.

Together we celebrate the hour,
In the midst of winter's power.
With every laugh and joyous song,
The heart of festivity beats strong.

Dreams Adrift in the Icy Cosmos

Dreams adrift, a cosmic swirl,
In icy realms, our hearts unfurl.
Stars above, they shine so bright,
Guiding us through the wintry night.

Snowflakes dance on whispered breeze,
Creating magic, putting minds at ease.
Gather 'round, let stories unfold,
In the warmth, our spirits bold.

Fires crackle, illuminating space,
Each flicker brings a smile to face.
Underneath the velvet sky,
Moments cherished as we fly.

With open hearts, we celebrate,
In this world, we navigate.
Joyful laughter fills the air,
In the cosmos, dreams laid bare.

Sparkling Frost in a Celestial Dream

Sparkling frost, a sight divine,
In the night, where stars align.
Each twinkle speaks of joy and cheer,
In celestial dreams, we draw near.

Underneath the blanket white,
We gather close, hearts ignite.
With every sip of cocoa warm,
Chasing away the winter's storm.

Voices blend like music sweet,
Sharing moments, so bittersweet.
Fires crackle, whispers blend,
In this season, love transcends.

Frosted pathways lead us on,
Together until the break of dawn.
In this festive, wondrous glow,
Magic lingers, hearts all aglow.

Stars Enshrined in Icy Splendor

Twinkling gems in velvet skies,
Glistening bright where silence lies.
Each diamond caught in winter's dream,
A radiant dance, a glimmering beam.

Snowflakes swirl in a joyful flight,
Painting the world in purest white.
Children laugh, their spirits soar,
As icy wonders beckon for more.

Lanterns glow in the frosty air,
Illuminating joy that's found everywhere.
Hot cocoa warms the chill of night,
While hugs and laughter feel just right.

Underneath the starry dome,
Hearts unite, together we roam.
In this place of wonder and cheer,
The magic of winter draws us near.

Frozen Nightfall and Cosmic Luminescence

The sun sinks low, a golden fade,
As twilight wraps the world in shade.
Stars awaken in cosmic flight,
Shimmering softly through the night.

Beneath the blanket of icy blue,
Dreams take shape in silver hue.
Silent whispers of a world so bright,
Painting hope in the shadowed night.

Frozen lakes mirror the sky,
Reflecting wonders that soar high.
As constellations begin to sing,
Melodies of joy that winter brings.

In every heart, the warmth ignites,
As we gather close on these starry nights.
Together we dream, together we beam,
In the frozen nightfall, we find our theme.

Whispering Winds of Cosmic Chill

Hushed whispers of the night behold,
A story of magic, timeless and bold.
Through pines and frost, soft breezes play,
As starlit dreams dance and sway.

The earth adorned in shimmering frost,
A glint of beauty, never lost.
Each gentle gust carries delight,
Awakening hearts with purest light.

Fires crackle, stories unfold,
Of winter's wonders forever told.
Adorned in bright, festive cheer,
Together we laugh, together we hear.

So let us gather, side by side,
In this wonder where dreams abide.
With whispers of joy and love to share,
A cosmic chill wraps us in care.

Celestial Icing

Underneath the frosted glow,
Celestial icing blankets below.
The night adorned in silver lace,
Holding dreams in a warm embrace.

Stars cascade in a crystal flurry,
Inviting hearts with a gentle hurry.
Each twinkle and flare a festive jest,
In the arms of winter, we find our nest.

Joyful voices fill the night,
Singing praises to the bright.
Hopeful wishes on icy air,
Hover like sparkles, grand and rare.

So gather 'round, let laughter span,
In this quiet, enchanted plan.
Celestial icing, a sight to behold,
A festive magic, more precious than gold.

A Frigid Dreamscape

In a frigid dreamscape, we find delight,
Where swirling snowflakes paint the night.
Echoes of laughter ride the breeze,
In the warmth of love, our hearts at ease.

Moonlit paths where shadows glide,
Adventurous spirits, nothing to hide.
Our hopes entwined in the frosty air,
Creating wishes beyond compare.

The twinkle of stars, a magical sight,
Illuminating our path, ever so bright.
In unison, we dance and sing,
As winter's charm begins to cling.

So treasure this time, let voices soar,
In this frigid dreamscape, we long for more.
Together we weave a tapestry grand,
A festive wonder, hand in hand.

Ethereal Frost and Cosmic Dreams

Under the glow of a silver moon,
Whispers of winter softly croon.
Stars twinkle like a crystal fair,
Frosted dreams linger in the air.

Snowflakes dance on a gentle breeze,
Spirits of joy float through the trees.
Laughter echoes, sweet and bright,
In the warm embrace of the night.

The world adorned in shimmering white,
Cozy hearts in the soft twilight.
Mirth and memories held so dear,
Ethereal warmth, the season near.

With each breath, the magic glows,
A festive charm that ever flows.
In this moment, all feels right,
Ethereal frost, our hearts ignite.

Chilling Radiance in the Night

In the stillness, silence reigns,
Chilling beauty, joy sustains.
Radiant lights in the frosty air,
Dancing shadows, we find our share.

Candles flicker, warmth ignites,
Glistening snowflakes, wondrous sights.
Under the arches of celestial glow,
Festive spirits begin to flow.

As laughter rings through the cool expanse,
Hearts entwined in a giddy dance.
Chill of winter, but hearts are warm,
In this night where dreams transform.

With every step, the season sings,
Of joyous times and precious things.
Embraced by night, we find our light,
Chilling radiance shines so bright.

Icy Shadows of the Cosmos

Icy shadows softly weave,
While cosmic wonders we conceive.
Stars adorned in a velvet sky,
Bidding us to dream and fly.

Frosted whispers fill the air,
Chill of joy is everywhere.
Laughter lights the frozen ground,
In this magic, love is found.

Through the night, we glide and swoon,
Under the watch of the glowing moon.
Moments sweet like sugarplums,
In the dark, our spirit hums.

Each fleeting glance, a festive spark,
Painting dreams in the tranquil dark.
In icy calm, our hearts combine,
Beneath the cosmos, we align.

Frosted Luminaries Above

Frosted luminaries, brightly shine,
Guiding souls through paths divine.
In the night, with hearts aglow,
Sharing secrets, gifts of snow.

Every twinkling star a wish,
Frosted wonders, sweet and delish.
Voices blend in a joyful choir,
Sparks of warmth, our hearts inspire.

Dreamers gather, tales unfold,
Festive stories, new and old.
In every glance, a story spun,
Under the frosted moon and sun.

As seasons dance and moments flare,
Frosted magic fills the air.
In this hour, let spirits soar,
With luminaries, forevermore.

www.ingramcontent.com/pod-product-compliance
Lightning Source LLC
Chambersburg PA
CBHW060408160125
20422CB00001B/195